444 + Fun Facts for Kids: Swimming Edition
Dive into Amazing Records, Epic Races, Incredible Swimmers & So Much More!
(The Ultimate Gift for Swimming Fans & Young Readers)?

Dr. Rabea Hadi

Board Certified Family Physician

Medical Scholar and Academic Trainer

Table of Contents:

Disclaimer

Information in this book is for education and entertainment purposes. For any mental, medical or financial advice, please consult a licensed professional. By reading this book, you agree that under no circumstances is the author responsible for any losses that are incurred due to using information within.

This is a work of fiction. Names, characters, places, and incidents either are products of the author's imagination or are used fictitiously. Any resemblance to actual persons, living or dead, events, or locales is coincidental.

I appreciate your constructive feedback at

mail@chooseyourquest.net

Review at Amazon & Goodreads.

Your Exclusive Adventure Awaits! (No Trolls Were Harmed in the Making of This Offer)

Dear Fellow Adventurer,

Firstly, kudos for bravely navigating the twists and turns of my book! As a reward (and because sending treasure chests via mail gets expensive), I'd like to offer you an **exclusive short story** set in the whimsical world of *Choose Your Quest*—available only to my most esteemed (and, dare I say, cleverest) readers? **<u>Disclaimer: This short story is intended for readers aged 13 and above</u>**.

<u>**Click here or scan the QR code**</u> to claim your free story and join our band of jesters!

By joining our quest, you may receive:

- **Early access** to new releases (beat the rush and the orcs!)
- **Exclusive content** not available anywhere else (not even from that sneaky goblin on the corner)

- **Insider updates** on upcoming projects
  (including secret plans to make dragons laugh)

This isn't just a book series; it's a mission to boost mental health through laughter and adventure. Each tale is crafted to tickle your funny bone, warm your heart, and maybe even make you snort in public (we won't tell).

Psst! As a subscriber, you might even get the inside scoop on why the dwarven jester crossed the road (spoiler: it involves a misplaced potion and a confused chicken).

If my book made you chuckle or grin. I'd be pleased. If you could leave a sparkling review on Amazon and Goodreads. Your words help fellow adventurers find their way to our joyful journey (and they may give me a legitimate reason to eat cake).

So, what are you waiting for? A dragon's invitation? Let's continue the quest together?

Introduction

Welcome to the World of Swimming Fun!

Hey there, swimming fan! Whether you're just learning the strokes or already taking laps like a pro, you're about to dive into a world packed with awesome facts, incredible records, and fascinating trivia—all about swimming!

Did you know that...

Swimming dates back thousands of years, evolving from natural ponds to Olympic-sized pools? From the science behind the perfect stroke to unbelievable endurance swims, this book will give you a peek into everything that makes swimming so exciting.

How to Read This Book

Each chapter covers a different part of the swimming world, from legendary races and top techniques to world-class pools and amazing records. And at the end of every chapter, you'll find three fun multiple-choice questions to test your swimming knowledge. Think you can swim your way to a perfect 444? Grab your goggles, adjust those swim caps, and let's jump in!

Get Ready to Become a Swimming Expert!

With 444 Fun Facts for Sports Kids: Swimming Edition, you'll uncover insights even serious swimmers might not know. So, dive in, take a deep breath, and let's explore the amazing, fact-filled world of swimming!

444+ SWIMMING FUN FACTS

chooseyourquest.net

Chapter 1: The Origins of Swimming

Fun Facts

1.   Swimming has been practiced for thousands of years, dating back to ancient Egypt.

2.   The first known swimming competition took place in Japan in the 1st century.

3.   Ancient Greek and Roman soldiers often swam as part of their training.

4.   The modern Olympic Games introduced swimming in 1896.

5.   Competitive swimming started in Europe in the early 1800s.

6.   Early swimming strokes included the sidestroke and breaststroke.

7.   The crawl, or freestyle, was introduced in the late 1800s.

8.   Swimming was added to the Women's Olympic program in 1912.

9.   The first swimming clubs were founded in London in the early 19th century.

10.   Swimming races were initially held in open water rather than pools.

11.   The ancient Japanese used swimming as a skill for survival and sport.

12.   Ancient Egyptian art shows figures swimming using a form of the breaststroke.

13.   Ancient Romans built public baths, where swimming was common.

14.   The freestyle stroke evolved from Native American swimming techniques.

15.   Swimming was introduced as a high school sport in the U.S. in the early 1900s.

16.   The first electric pool lighting was used in 1908 for nighttime swimming.

17.   Swimming became a popular leisure activity in Europe during the Renaissance.

18.   Early competitions were held over various distances, from 100 yards to several miles.

19.   The first official swimming world championship took place in 1973.

20.   Olympic swimming started with just freestyle and breaststroke events.

21.   The butterfly stroke was originally developed as a variation of the breaststroke.

22.   Swimming became an official part of the Commonwealth Games in 1930.

23.   Swimming pools were added to schools and universities in the early 20th century.

24.   The backstroke was introduced in the Olympics in 1900.

25.   Today, swimming is one of the most popular sports worldwide, with millions participating.

End-of-Chapter Quiz

1.   In which year did swimming become part of the modern Olympic Games?

- A) 1896

- B) 1900

- C) 1920

- D) 1912

Answer: A) 1896

2.   Which stroke evolved from Native American techniques?

- A) Breaststroke

- B) Butterfly

- C) Freestyle

- D) Sidestroke

Answer: C) Freestyle

3.   Where did the first known swimming competition take place?

- A) Greece

- B) Rome

- C) Japan

- D) Egypt

Answer: C) Japan

STAY SAFE THIS SUMMER

SUMMER SAFETY TIPS

BE SUN SMART

Wear sunscreen and protective clothing – including sunglasses – to protect against UV rays. And don't forget a hat!

Seek shade under a tree or umbrella.

STAY HYDRATED

Drink water throughout the day to replace fluid lost to sweat & heat.

READ THE SIGNS

Look for safety signs at the beach and swim between flags or under the watch of lifeguards.

TAKE A FRIEND

Swim with a friend, never alone.

17

Chapter 2: Swimming Strokes and Techniques

Fun Facts

1. There are four main strokes in competitive swimming: freestyle, backstroke, breaststroke, and butterfly.

2. Freestyle, also known as the front crawl, is the fastest swimming stroke.

3. Backstroke is the only stroke where swimmers lie on their backs.

4. Breaststroke is often considered one of the oldest swimming strokes.

5. The butterfly stroke requires both arms to move symmetrically.

6. Freestyle races can be as short as 50 meters or as long as 1,500 meters.

7. Breaststroke is known for its unique frog-like kick.

8. The butterfly stroke is also called "fly" for short.

9. Backstroke races are typically shorter than freestyle events.

10. In the individual medley, swimmers compete using all four strokes in one race.

11. The freestyle stroke allows swimmers to choose any stroke they prefer.

12. In breaststroke, both arms move simultaneously in a circular motion.

13. The butterfly stroke requires a powerful dolphin kick.

14. The freestyle stroke was inspired by the Native American "front crawl."

15. Backstroke races begin with a unique start, with swimmers pushing off on their backs.

16. The butterfly stroke demands strong core muscles for balance.

17. In a relay race, four swimmers each swim a segment of the race.

18. Freestyle relays are often the most exciting events in competitions.

19. Breaststroke is known for being slower but very energy-efficient.

20. The flip turn is a technique used in freestyle and backstroke for faster turns.

21. Butterfly is considered the most challenging stroke due to its demanding technique.

22. Breaststroke requires precise timing between the kick and arm pull.

23. The individual medley combines all four strokes in one race.

24. Swimmers often have a preferred stroke where they excel.

25. Competitive swimmers practice each stroke's techniques for speed and efficiency.

End-of-Chapter Quiz

1.   Which stroke allows swimmers to lie on their backs?

- A) Freestyle

- B) Breaststroke

- C) Backstroke

- D) Butterfly

Answer: C) Backstroke

2.   What is another name for the freestyle stroke?

- A) Sidestroke

- B) Front crawl

- C) Back crawl

- D) Dolphin stroke

Answer: B) Front crawl

3.   How many strokes are used in an individual medley race?

- A) One

- B) Two

- C) Three
- D) Four

Answer: D) Four

Chapter 3: Olympic Swimming Legends

Fun Facts

1.   The first Olympic swimming events were held in open water.

2.   Olympic swimming is now one of the most-watched events in the Summer Games.

3.   Swimmers can compete in up to seven events in the Olympics.

4.   The Olympic pool is 50 meters long, also known as a "long course" pool.

5.   Olympic swimmers train year-round to prepare for the Games.

6.   Each Olympic swimming event has preliminaries, semifinals, and a final round.

7.   Winning an Olympic gold medal is considered the ultimate achievement for swimmers.

8.   Olympic swimmers have specific routines and rituals before races.

9.   The backstroke and breaststroke were both included in early Olympic competitions.

10.   Relay races add a thrilling team element to the Olympic swimming program.

11.   Olympic records are tracked for each event and stroke.

12.   Some Olympic swimmers specialize in a specific stroke, while others compete in multiple.

13.   The butterfly was officially introduced to the Olympics in 1956.

14.   Freestyle events range from 50 meters up to the 1,500 meters at the Olympics.

15.   The "medley relay" includes all four strokes, swum by four different team members.

16.   Olympic swimmers are known for their strict diets and intense workout schedules.

17.   In the Olympics, each country is allowed to enter two swimmers per event.

18.	The Olympic Games have seen many thrilling photo-finishes in swimming.

19.	Swimmers use specific warm-up routines to stay loose before races.

20.	The starting block design has evolved to improve swimmers' starts.

21.	Some swimmers have competed in multiple Olympic Games over their careers.

22.	Swimmers are disqualified if they start early, known as a "false start."

23.	The 4x100m freestyle relay is one of the most competitive Olympic swimming events.

24.	Olympic pools are designed to reduce water turbulence for faster races.

25.	Olympic swimming has inspired millions worldwide to take up the sport.

End-of-Chapter Quiz

1.   **How long is an Olympic-sized swimming pool?**

- A) 25 meters

- B) 50 meters

- C) 100 meters

- D) 200 meters

Answer: B) 50 meters

2.   **In what year was the butterfly stroke introduced to the Olympics?**

- A) 1924

- B) 1956

- C) 1968

- D) 1980

Answer: B) 1956

3.   **What is the term for starting a race early in swimming?**

- A) False start

26

- **B) Early swim**

- **C) Pre-jump**

- **D) Fast flip**

Answer: A) False start

Chapter 4: Famous Swimming Pools Around the World

Fun Facts

1.   The Bondi Icebergs Pool in Australia sits right beside the ocean.

2.   The Infinity Pool at Marina Bay Sands in Singapore overlooks the city skyline.

3.   The Piscine Molitor in Paris is famous for its luxurious design.

4.   The London Aquatics Centre was built for the 2012 Olympics.

5.   Blue Lagoon in Iceland has geothermal waters perfect for relaxing swims.

6.   The Y-40 pool in Italy is the deepest indoor pool, reaching 131 feet.

7.   The Nemo 33 pool in Belgium is also known for its deep diving area.

8.   The Badeschiff in Berlin is a floating pool in the River Spree.

9.   San Alfonso del Mar in Chile is one of the world's largest outdoor pools.

10.   The Olympic Pool in Munich, Germany, was built for the 1972 Olympics.

11.   The Hearst Castle Pool in California is known for its Roman-inspired design.

12.   Crystal Lagoon in Islamic Egypt is a giant pool built near a desert.

13.   The Homestead Crater in Utah is a natural geothermal pool inside a limestone rock.

14.   Gellért Baths in Hungary combines history with thermal waters.

15.   The Red Pool in Thailand has red-tiled walls, creating a unique look.

16.   The Floating Pool Lady in New York City is on a barge in the East River.

17.   The Sky Pool in London is a glass pool that bridges two buildings.

18.   The Amangiri Pool in Utah blends with the surrounding desert landscape.

19.   The Weird Pool in Zambia lets swimmers float near Victoria Falls.

20.   The Lava Pools in Portugal were formed naturally by volcanic rock.

21.   The Piraeus Pool in Greece has a view of the Mediterranean Sea.

22.   The Hanging Gardens Pool in Bali is surrounded by lush rainforest.

23.   Thermae Bath Spa in the UK has mineral-rich waters.

24.   The Sunway Lagoon Wave Pool in Malaysia is one of the largest wave pools.

25.   Swimming pools are built in all shapes, sizes, and locations around the world.

End-of-Chapter Quiz

1.   Where is the famous Bondi Icebergs Pool located?

- A) New York

- B) Paris

- C) Berlin

- D) Australia

Answer: D) Australia

2.   Which pool in Italy is known as the world's deepest indoor pool?

- A) Nemo 33

- B) Y-40

- C) Marina Bay Sands

- D) Blue Lagoon

Answer: B) Y-40

3.   What is unique about the Floating Pool Lady in New York City?

- A) It's on a barge in the East River

- **B) It has glass walls**

- **C) It's a hot spring**

- **D) It's located in Central Park**

Answer: A) It's on a barge in the East River

Chapter 5: Unusual Swimming World Records

Fun Facts

1. The longest swim without flippers is 139 miles, held by Veljko Rogošić.

2. The fastest 50-meter swim was completed in under 21 seconds.

3. The most people swimming in a relay is over 5,000, set in Italy.

4. The youngest competitive swimmer was only four years old.

5. The longest time underwater without breathing is 24 minutes.

6. The oldest competitive swimmer was 101 years old.

7. The record for the most medals won in a single Olympics is held by one swimmer.

8. The fastest 100-meter freestyle time is under 47 seconds.

9.   The highest dive into water was from a height of 192 feet.

10.   The longest distance underwater with one breath is over 800 feet.

11.   The longest time treading water is over 85 hours.

12.   The most laps swum in 24 hours is over 100 miles.

13.   The record for the longest pool float train involved over 500 floats.

14.   The biggest swimming lesson involved over 36,000 participants.

15.   The longest time swimming in open water is more than 80 hours.

16.   The fastest 200-meter freestyle is under 1 minute and 43 seconds.

17.   The highest swimming pool is in Dubai, 1,000 feet above the ground.

18.   The record for most swimming caps worn at once is over 100.

19.   The longest distance swimming on a paddleboard is over 500 miles.

20.   The deepest underwater swim with a single breath reached 831 feet.

21.   The record for the most people swimming with glow sticks is over 2,000.

22.   The fastest 50-meter butterfly is under 23 seconds.

23.   The world's largest swimming pool is over 3,000 feet long.

24.   The longest time swimming backward was 19 hours.

25.   World records in swimming are continually set and broken each year.

End-of-Chapter Quiz

1. **What is the longest swim without flippers on record?**

- **A) 50 miles**

- **B) 100 miles**

- **C) 139 miles**

- **D) 200 miles**

Answer: C) 139 miles

2. **What is the longest time spent treading water?**

- **A) 10 hours**

- **B) 24 hours**

- **C) 50 hours**

- **D) 85 hours**

Answer: D) 85 hours

3. **How many people participated in the largest swimming lesson?**

- **A) 5,000**

- **B) 10,000**

- **C) 20,000**

- **D) 36,000**

Answer: D) 36,000

Chapter 6: Famous Swimmers and Their Accomplishments

Fun Facts

1.	Michael Phelps is known for winning the most Olympic medals in history.

2.	Mark Spitz was a top swimmer, winning seven gold medals in one Olympics.

3.	Caeleb Dressel is known for his powerful sprints and record-breaking times.

4.	Ian Thorpe, also known as "The Thorpedo," won multiple Olympic medals for Australia.

5.	Matt Biondi won 11 Olympic medals during his swimming career.

6.	Ryan Lochte holds multiple world records in swimming.

7.	Grant Hackett was known for his endurance in long-distance swimming.

8.	Nathan Adrian is recognized for his relay performances in the Olympics.

9.	Kosuke Kitajima made history in the breaststroke for Japan.

10.	Roland Schoeman from South Africa holds records in butterfly and freestyle.

11.	César Cielo of Brazil set world records in sprint freestyle events.

12.	Sun Yang is known for his achievements in distance freestyle events.

13.	Gary Hall Jr. won gold in freestyle relays for the United States.

14.	Pieter van den Hoogenband set multiple records in the early 2000s.

15.	Alexander Popov, known as "The Russian Rocket," excelled in freestyle.

16.	Adam Peaty is famous for his world records in breaststroke.

17.	Florent Manaudou of France is a top competitor in sprint freestyle.

18.	Chad le Clos won gold in the 200m butterfly for South Africa.

19.   Yannick Agnel from France won gold in freestyle events.

20.   Matt Grevers is known for his achievements in backstroke.

21.   Kosuke Hagino from Japan is known for his versatility in multiple strokes.

22.   Park Tae-hwan made history as a top swimmer from South Korea.

23.   Anthony Ervin won Olympic medals 16 years apart.

24.   Dmitriy Balandin was the first Olympic swimming gold medalist from Kazakhstan.

25.   Famous swimmers inspire young athletes and set records that push the sport forward.

End-of-Chapter Quiz

1.   Who holds the record for winning the most Olympic medals in history?

- A) Mark Spitz

- B) Ian Thorpe

- C) Michael Phelps

- D) Ryan Lochte

Answer: C) Michael Phelps

2.   What is Ian Thorpe's nickname?

- A) The Rocket

- B) The Thorpedo

- C) The Missile

- D) The Machine

Answer: B) The Thorpedo

3.   Who set multiple world records in breaststroke?

- A) Grant Hackett

- **B) Alexander Popov**

- **C) Adam Peaty**

- **D) Chad le Clos**

Answer: C) Adam Peaty

Chapter 7: Swimming Techniques and Training

Fun Facts

1.   Competitive swimmers train six days a week to stay in peak condition.

2.   Swim coaches focus on both technique and endurance in training.

3.   Swimmers often practice "dryland" exercises like running and weightlifting.

4.   Flip turns in freestyle help swimmers maintain speed during turns.

5.   Dolphin kicks are used in butterfly and streamline swimming for extra propulsion.

6.   Swimmers use "pull buoys" to work on upper-body strength.

7.   Swimmers practice breathing on both sides, called "bilateral breathing."

8.   The butterfly kick is known for its strength and speed.

9.   Resistance training helps swimmers build explosive power.

10.   Tapering is a period when swimmers reduce training before competitions.

11.   Swimmers often practice in open water to adapt to different environments.

12.   Swimmers build core strength to stabilize their movements in the water.

13.   Freestyle kick drills improve leg speed and endurance.

14.   Swimmers use paddles to increase water resistance in training.

15.   Swimmers practice long-distance sets to build endurance.

16.   Technique drills focus on improving stroke efficiency.

17.   The "catch" phase is when swimmers pull the most water with their arms.

18.   Streamline position helps reduce drag and improve speed.

19.   Swimmers often set personal goals to track improvement.

20.   Recovery is important, including proper nutrition and rest.

21.   Swimmers wear resistance bands to increase difficulty in drills.

22.   Breath control exercises help swimmers manage oxygen during races.

23.   Swimmers use a metronome to improve stroke rhythm.

24.   Visualization techniques are used to mentally prepare for races.

25.   Coaches analyze stroke video footage to help swimmers refine technique.

End-of-Chapter Quiz

1.   What is "tapering" in swimming?

•   **A) Increasing training intensity**

•   **B) Reducing training before a competition**

•   **C) Changing swim strokes**

•   **D) Practicing only in open water**

Answer: B) Reducing training before a competition

2.   What does "bilateral breathing" mean?

•   **A) Breathing only on the left side**

•   **B) Breathing only on the right side**

•   **C) Breathing on both sides**

•   **D) Holding your breath**

Answer: C) Breathing on both sides

3. Which phase of the stroke pulls the most water?

- A) Glide

- B) Catch

- C) Finish

- D) Recovery

Answer: B) Catch

Chapter 8: Unique Open-Water Swimming Feats

Fun Facts

1. Open-water swimming involves races in natural bodies of water like oceans and lakes.

2. The English Channel swim is a famous open-water challenge, covering 21 miles.

3. Some open-water swimmers face jellyfish stings while completing long swims.

4. Swimming around Manhattan Island in New York is a popular open-water race.

5. Ice swimming is a type of open-water swim in freezing temperatures.

6. Open-water races can be affected by currents, waves, and tides.

7. Swimmers crossing the English Channel deal with cold water and strong tides.

8.   The Catalina Channel swim is a 20-mile race off the coast of California.

9.   Lake Zurich in Switzerland hosts one of the world's oldest open-water swims.

10.   Swimmers have crossed from Cuba to Florida without a shark cage.

11.   The Triple Crown of Open Water Swimming includes three famous swims.

12.   Some swimmers use grease on their skin to protect against cold.

13.   Open-water races may require wetsuits for warmth and buoyancy.

14.   The Alcatraz swim involves swimming from Alcatraz Island to San Francisco.

15.   Open-water swims can last several hours, requiring high endurance.

16.   Swimmers are often escorted by boats for safety.

17.   Freshwater swims are more challenging due to the lack of buoyancy.

18.   The Strait of Gibraltar swim is a 9-mile route between Europe and Africa.

19.   Open-water swimmers must navigate without lanes or walls.

20.   Some open-water races reach distances of up to 25 kilometers.

21.   Swimmers may encounter fish and marine life during races.

22.   Swimmers use GPS to map out courses for long-distance swims.

23.   Open-water training includes adapting to different temperatures.

24.   The "Channel Swim" record for the English Channel is under 7 hours.

25.   Open-water swimming requires both physical and mental strength.

End-of-Chapter Quiz

1.   What is the distance of the English Channel swim?

- A) 10 miles

- B) 15 miles

- C) 21 miles

- D) 30 miles

Answer: C) 21 miles

2.   What is ice swimming?

- A) Swimming with an ice cube

- B) Swimming in freezing water

- C) Swimming in tropical waters

- D) Swimming while holding your breath

Answer: B) Swimming in freezing water

3.   Which swim is part of the Triple Crown of Open Water Swimming?

- A) Lake Zurich swim
- B) English Channel swim
- C) Mediterranean swim
- D) Caribbean swim

Answer: B) English Channel swim

Chapter 9: The Science of Swimming

Fun Facts

1.   Buoyancy allows swimmers to float on water with less effort.

2.   Water resistance, or drag, slows swimmers down in the pool.

3.   Swimmers reduce drag by maintaining a streamlined position.

4.   Hydrodynamics is the study of water flow, important in swimming.

5.   Fast swimsuits are designed to minimize drag and improve speed.

6.   Swimmers create a "wake" in the water, similar to boats.

7.   Arm and leg muscles are critical for powerful strokes.

8.   Swimmers practice kicking to improve propulsion.

9.   The human body is naturally buoyant due to its composition.

10. The density of water makes it more resistant than air.

11. Water temperature affects swimmers' endurance and speed.

12. Swimmers keep their heads down in freestyle to reduce drag.

13. Swimmers use rotational movements to propel themselves.

14. Efficient breathing techniques improve oxygen flow to muscles.

15. Flip turns reduce time in races by allowing quick direction changes.

16. Swimmers maintain balance by using core muscles.

17. Swimmers use large muscle groups to generate forward movement.

18. Fast suits are made from materials that reduce water absorption.

19. Breath control is essential in managing energy and speed.

20. Different strokes use muscles in distinct ways.

21. Swimmers push off the pool wall with a strong start for momentum.

22.   Training at high altitudes can improve swimming endurance.

23.   Pool lane lines are designed to reduce water turbulence.

24.   Swimmers use "sculling" movements to improve hand positioning.

25.   The science behind swimming helps athletes optimize their performance.

End-of-Chapter Quiz

1.   What is water resistance also known as?

- **A) Buoyancy**
- **B) Density**
- **C) Drag**
- **D) Flow**

Answer: C) Drag

2.   What helps swimmers stay afloat?

- **A) Density**
- **B) Drag**
- **C) Buoyancy**
- **D) Friction**

Answer: C) Buoyancy

3.   What is the purpose of lane lines in a pool?

- **A) To keep swimmers in place**

- B) To reduce water turbulence

- C) To add color

- D) To make races harder

Answer: B) To reduce water turbulence

Chapter 10: Swimming Records and Achievements

Fun Facts

1. The record for the fastest 50-meter freestyle is under 21 seconds.

2. The 100-meter freestyle record is under 47 seconds.

3. Michael Phelps holds the record for the most Olympic swimming medals.

4. The longest swim in open water was 139 miles.

5. The world record for the fastest 200-meter butterfly is under 1 minute, 51 seconds.

6. The youngest swimmer to set a world record was just 14 years old.

7. The fastest 400-meter freestyle record is under 3 minutes, 41 seconds.

8. The highest swim pool is on the 57th floor of a Singapore hotel.

9. The 50-meter breaststroke record is under 25 seconds.

10. Some swimming records have stood for over a decade.

11. The 800-meter freestyle world record is under 7 minutes, 33 seconds.

12. The most gold medals won in a single Olympics by a swimmer is eight.

13. Swimmers often specialize in one stroke to break records.

14. The longest distance underwater on a single breath is over 800 feet.

15. The 200-meter backstroke record is under 1 minute, 52 seconds.

16. Olympic swimming pools are exactly 50 meters in length.

17. The record for the most back-to-back Olympic appearances by a swimmer is six.

18. The 400-meter medley combines all four strokes in one race.

19. The 100-meter breaststroke world record is under 57 seconds.

20. The 1,500-meter freestyle record is under 14 minutes, 31 seconds.

21. The 200-meter freestyle record is under 1 minute, 43 seconds.

22.   Relay teams hold unique records for combined team performances.

23.   The fastest flip turn is completed in under 1 second.

24.   The 50-meter backstroke record is under 24 seconds.

25.   Swimming records are set and broken by athletes worldwide every year.

End-of-Chapter Quiz

1. **What is the fastest 50-meter freestyle time?**

- A) Under 20 seconds

- B) Under 21 seconds

- C) Under 22 seconds

- D) Under 23 seconds

Answer: B) Under 21 seconds

2. **How long is an Olympic swimming pool?**

- A) 25 meters

- B) 50 meters

- C) 100 meters

- D) 75 meters

Answer: B) 50 meters

3. **Which swim race combines all four strokes?**

- A) Freestyle

- B) Butterfly

- **C) Medley**
- **D) Breaststroke**

Answer: C) Medley

Chapter 11: Swimming Technology and Equipment

Fun Facts

1.   Fast suits are made from materials that minimize water absorption.

2.   Goggles were first allowed in Olympic swimming in 1976.

3.   Swim caps reduce drag and help streamline swimmers' heads.

4.   Some swimmers use earplugs to prevent water from entering their ears.

5.   Underwater cameras capture swimmers' techniques for analysis.

6.   Advanced swimsuits are designed to improve buoyancy.

7.   Flip turn sensors help swimmers practice timing.

8.   Swimmers use heart rate monitors during training.

9.   Kickboards help swimmers practice leg strength.

10.   Paddles add resistance in water to build upper-body strength.

11.   Handheld kick counters help swimmers track their lap counts.

12.   Weighted pull buoys assist in training different muscle groups.

13.   Swim watches are used to time laps and track distance.

14.   Swim caps are made from silicone or latex for comfort and speed.

15.   Resistance cords help swimmers build strength in specific strokes.

16.   Swimmers train with snorkels to improve breathing technique.

17.   High-tech pools have temperature control for ideal conditions.

18.   Lane lines in pools help reduce turbulence.

19.   Swim fins improve ankle flexibility and leg strength.

20.   Touchpads at pool walls electronically record swimmers' times.

21.   Swimmers use foam rollers for post-training recovery.

22.	Swim goggles with anti-fog lenses keep vision clear underwater.

23.	Parachutes create drag for resistance training in the pool.

24.	Body markers are used to measure performance during training.

25.	Technology continues to push the limits of performance in swimming.

End-of-Chapter Quiz

1. **When were goggles first allowed in Olympic swimming?**

- **A) 1960**

- **B) 1972**

- **C) 1976**

- **D) 1980**

Answer: C) 1976

2. **What is the purpose of a swim cap?**

- **A) To keep hair dry**

- **B) To reduce drag**

- **C) To add weight**

- **D) To warm the head**

Answer: B) To reduce drag

3. **What device is used to record swimmers' times at the pool wall?**

- **A) Stopwatch**

- **B) Timer block**

- C) Touchpad
- D) Lap counter

Answer: C) Touchpad

Chapter 12: Wrong Swimming Traditions

Facts

1.   Swimmers often splash themselves with water before races for comfort.

2.   Many swimmers wear lucky goggles or suits during races.

3.   Swimmers have pre-race rituals, like specific warm-ups or stretches.

4.   Some swimmers listen to music to stay focused before a race.

5.   Celebratory pool jumps are common after a big win.

6.   Swimmers may have a specific breathing pattern for good luck.

7.   Shaving body hair before races is a common practice for reducing drag.

8.   Swimmers give "high fives" to teammates after races.

9.   Wearing team colors is a tradition at major competitions.

10. Swimmers often perform dryland stretches as a warm-up routine.

11. Many swimmers develop superstitions about their swim caps.

12. Standing on the block with a specific stance is a pre-race habit.

13. After a big race, swimmers might throw their caps into the crowd.

14. Pre-race visualization is common to mentally prepare.

15. Swimmers sometimes splash opponents to create playful rivalry.

16. Many teams have a specific chant or cheer before competing.

17. Swimmers might avoid wearing new suits on race day.

18. Celebratory water splashes are common for team victories.

19. Some swimmers use specific breathing exercises to stay calm.

20. Swimmers may wear multiple caps for better speed.

21. Teams often take group photos after competition victories.

22. Waving to the crowd is a common post-race tradition.

23. Many swimmers bring lucky towels to every race.

24. Swimmers sometimes give autographs on caps after big races.

25. These traditions are wrong and don't add to the competitive swimming.

End-of-Chapter Quiz

1.   **What is one common pre-race ritual for swimmers?**

- **A) Running**

- **B) Splashing themselves with water**

- **C) Eating fast food**

- **D) Wearing casual clothes**

Answer: B) Splashing themselves with water

2.   **What is a reason swimmers shave body hair before a race?**

- **A) For fashion**

- **B) To reduce drag**

- **C) To stay warm**

- **D) To impress the crowd**

Answer: B) To reduce drag

3.   **Why might swimmers wear multiple caps?**

- **A) For better speed**

- **B) To make a statement**
- **C) To hide hair color**
- **D) For extra warmth**

Answer: A) For better speed

Chapter 13: Famous Swimming Coaches

Fun Facts

1. Bob Bowman coached Michael Phelps to Olympic success.

2. Doc Counsilman was known for his innovative swim training techniques.

3. Eddie Reese has led the University of Texas swimming team to multiple titles.

4. Bill Sweetenham has coached swimmers in five different countries.

5. David Marsh is a highly respected coach in the U.S. swimming community.

6. Gregg Troy coached Ryan Lochte and the U.S. Olympic team.

7. Jon Urbanchek was known for his dedication to developing young talent.

8. Ray Looze is known for his unique training programs at Indiana University.

9. Richard Quick coached multiple Olympic swimmers to success.

10. Mike Bottom is celebrated for his sprint-focused swim training.

11. Bob Gillett pioneered advanced butterfly techniques.

12. Yuri Sugiyama has coached several top swimmers at Stanford.

13. Jack Bauerle has a long history with the University of Georgia swim team.

14. Gregg Troy developed a strong swim program at the University of Florida.

15. Australian coach Denis Cotterell trained long-distance swimmer Grant Hackett.

16. Sergio Lopez has coached swimmers from Spain, Singapore, and the U.S.

17. Rowdy Gaines is known as a coach and swimming broadcaster.

18. Teri McKeever was the first woman to coach the U.S. Olympic swim team.

19. Steve Furniss was an Olympic swimmer and coach for young swimmers.

20. Dave Salo is known for his innovative training methods.

21. Frank Busch coached the University of Arizona to NCAA championships.

22. Dick Jochums focused on mental resilience in swimming.

23.   Doug Frost developed multiple training plans for elite swimmers.

24.   Bob Bowman emphasizes strong mental preparation for competitions.

25.   Great coaches help swimmers reach their full potential and inspire others.

End-of-Chapter Quiz

1.   **Who coached Michael Phelps to his Olympic success?**

- **A) Eddie Reese**

- **B) Doc Counsilman**

- **C) Bob Bowman**

- **D) David Marsh**

Answer: C) Bob Bowman

2.   **Which coach is known for sprint-focused swim training?**

- **A) Mike Bottom**

- **B) Gregg Troy**

- **C) Jack Bauerle**

- **D) Richard Quick**

Answer: A) Mike Bottom

3.   **What is one quality great coaches bring to their swimmers?**

- **A) Strict rules**

- **B) Innovative techniques**

- **C) Focus on only one stroke**

- **D) Avoiding competitions**

Answer: B) Innovative techniques

Chapter 14: The Physics of Swimming

Fun Facts

1. Buoyancy is a force that helps swimmers float.

2. Drag slows down a swimmer as they move through water.

3. The streamlined position helps reduce drag.

4. Swimmers displace water to propel forward.

5. Hydrodynamics is the study of water flow, crucial in swimming.

6. Water density is greater than air, providing resistance.

7. Faster strokes require powerful arm and leg movements.

8. Kicking generates lift and helps maintain speed.

9. The backstroke has lower drag due to body position.

10. Waves in the pool can slow swimmers down.

11. Lane dividers help reduce turbulence.

12. Swimmers use core strength to stabilize movement.

13. Flip turns reduce time by keeping momentum.

14. Swimmers' body shapes affect how they move through water.

15. Drag suits increase resistance to build strength in training.

16. Goggles improve visibility, affecting a swimmer's direction.

17. Water's surface tension affects strokes like freestyle.

18. Underwater dolphin kicks create a wave motion for speed.

19. Swimmers minimize drag by keeping elbows high in strokes.

20. The angle of entry in the pool affects swimmers' speed.

21. Streamline drills train swimmers to glide through water efficiently.

22.   Resistance bands add drag to training for power.

23.   Swimmers reduce resistance by shaving body hair.

24.   Hand positioning is crucial for an effective "catch" phase.

25.   Understanding physics helps swimmers refine techniques for better speed.

End-of-Chapter Quiz

1. **What is buoyancy?**

- **A) Force that slows swimmers**
- **B) Force that helps swimmers float**
- **C) Speed technique**
- **D) Training tool**

Answer: B) Force that helps swimmers float

2. **What helps reduce drag in the backstroke?**

- **A) High kicking**
- **B) Body position**
- **C) Arm pull**
- **D) Lower breathing rate**

Answer: B) Body position

3. **Why do swimmers perform streamline drills?**

- **A) To improve breathing**
- **B) To improve glide efficiency**

- C) To create more waves
- D) To add drag

Answer: B) To improve glide efficiency

Chapter 15: Swimming Legends in History

Fun Facts

1.   Johnny Weissmuller was the first swimmer to break the one-minute mark in the 100m freestyle.

2.   Mark Spitz won seven gold medals in one Olympics, a record at the time.

3.   Michael Phelps set an Olympic record with eight gold medals in 2008.

4.   Don Schollander was the first swimmer to win four golds in one Olympics.

5.   Ian Thorpe, known as "The Thorpedo," was a champion from Australia.

6.   Alexander Popov is remembered for his achievements in freestyle.

7.   Matt Biondi won 11 Olympic medals during his career.

8.   Gary Hall Jr. was known for his sprint freestyle prowess.

9.   Pieter van den Hoogenband set records in the early 2000s.

10.   Kosuke Kitajima dominated in breaststroke for Japan.

11.   Rowdy Gaines set world records in freestyle in the 1980s.

12.   Caeleb Dressel is a current record-holder and champion sprinter.

13.   Greg Louganis was a legendary diver who started as a swimmer.

14.   Tom Dolan won Olympic gold in the medley races.

15.   Ryan Lochte set multiple world records in individual medleys.

16.   Matt Grevers was a champion in backstroke events.

17.   Tom Malchow excelled in butterfly races for the U.S.

18.   Dave Wilkie made history in breaststroke for Great Britain.

19.   Aaron Peirsol was known for his dominance in backstroke.

20.   Duncan Armstrong surprised the world with his freestyle gold.

21.   Cesar Cielo became a sprinting legend from Brazil.

22.   Chad le Clos won gold in the 200m butterfly.

23.   Florent Manaudou is a top French swimmer and sprinter.

24.   Shane Gould was a young champion who broke records.

25.   These legends inspire future generations of swimmers around the world.

End-of-Chapter Quiz

1.   Who was the first swimmer to break the one-minute mark in the 100m freestyle?

- A) Mark Spitz

- B) Johnny Weissmuller

- C) Michael Phelps

- D) Ian Thorpe

Answer: B) Johnny Weissmuller

2.   Who won seven gold medals in a single Olympics before Michael Phelps?

- A) Matt Biondi

- B) Gary Hall Jr.

- C) Alexander Popov

- D) Mark Spitz

Answer: D) Mark Spitz

3.   Which swimmer is known as "The Thorpedo"?

- A) Ian Thorpe

- **B) Alexander Popov**

- **C) Caeleb Dressel**

- **D) Ryan Lochte**

Answer: A) Ian Thorpe

Chapter 16: World-Class Swimming Competitions

Fun Facts

1.   The Olympic Games is the pinnacle of international swimming competitions.

2.   The FINA World Championships host the best swimmers globally every two years.

3.   The Pan Pacific Championships feature top swimmers from Pacific Rim countries.

4.   The European Championships showcase the best of Europe's swimmers.

5.   The Commonwealth Games include athletes from countries formerly in the British Empire.

6.   The Asian Games have a strong swimming program for Asia's top athletes.

7.   The NCAA Championships are major events for U.S. college swimmers.

8.   The U.S. Nationals serve as a qualification for Olympic and international teams.

9.   Swimming World Cup events allow swimmers to earn points at various meets.

10.   The Youth Olympic Games feature young swimming talent from around the world.

11.   Australia's Swimming Championships are highly competitive in the sport.

12.   The Japan Swimming Championships showcase top swimmers in Japan.

13.   The Mediterranean Games bring together athletes from Mediterranean countries.

14.   The All-Africa Games highlight swimmers from across Africa.

15.   The South American Championships promote top swimming talent in the continent.

16.   The World Masters Championships include athletes of all ages in swimming events.

17.   The Mare Nostrum Series in Europe attracts top international swimmers.

18.   The Central American and Caribbean Games feature top regional athletes.

19.   FINA Short Course Championships are held in 25-meter pools.

20.   The Goodwill Games were held to encourage international sportsmanship.

21.   The British Swimming Championships are top events in the UK.

22.   The Southeast Asian Games have a strong swimming program.

23.   The LEN Cup in Europe allows top swimmers to compete regionally.

24.   The Gulf Swimming Championships feature talent from the Gulf region.

25.   These competitions are where records are set and legends are made.

End-of-Chapter Quiz

1.   What is the highest international competition for swimmers?

- A) FINA World Cup

- B) Pan Pacific Championships

- C) Olympic Games

- D) Commonwealth Games

Answer: C) Olympic Games

2.   What is the length of the pool in the FINA Short Course Championships?

- A) 50 meters

- B) 25 meters

- C) 100 meters

- D) 75 meters

Answer: B) 25 meters

3.   Which event features college swimmers in the U.S.?

- A) Commonwealth Games

- B) Youth Olympics

- C) NCAA Championships
- D) World Masters Championships

Answer: C) NCAA Championships

Chapter 17: Open-Water Swimming Challenges

Fun Facts

1.   Open-water swimming is held in natural bodies like oceans, rivers, and lakes.

2.   The English Channel is a popular open-water challenge covering 21 miles.

3.   Swimmers face currents, tides, and marine life in open-water races.

4.   The Strait of Gibraltar swim connects Europe and Africa across 9 miles.

5.   The Alcatraz swim takes athletes from Alcatraz Island to San Francisco.

6.   Lake Zurich in Switzerland hosts a famous open-water swimming event.

7.   Catalina Channel is a challenging swim near California's coast.

8.   The Rottnest Channel Swim in Australia covers 12 miles.

9.   Ice swimming is an extreme form of open-water swimming in cold waters.

10. Swimmers often wear wetsuits in colder water for insulation.

11. The Manhattan Island Marathon Swim circles New York City's island.

12. The Maui Channel Swim is held between islands in Hawaii.

13. Some open-water races cover distances up to 25 kilometers.

14. Open-water swimming can be affected by weather changes.

15. Swimmers in open water navigate without pool walls or lane lines.

16. Safety boats escort swimmers in long open-water races.

17. The Triple Crown of Open Water Swimming includes the English Channel, Catalina Channel, and Manhattan Island swims.

18. Marathon swimming involves distances over 10 kilometers.

19. The North Channel swim is known for its cold temperatures and jellyfish.

20. Open-water swimmers train in lakes, rivers, and oceans.

21. Swimmers use sighting techniques to stay on course.

22.   The Zurich Lake swim is one of the world's oldest open-water races.

23.   Some open-water races involve feeding stations for swimmers.

24.   The Channel Swimming Association regulates English Channel swims.

25.   Open-water swimming requires strength, endurance, and navigation skills.

End-of-Chapter Quiz

1.   What is a well-known open-water swim from Alcatraz Island?

- **A) Catalina Channel**

- **B) Rottnest Channel**

- **C) Alcatraz Swim**

- **D) North Channel**

Answer: C) Alcatraz Swim

2.   What does the Triple Crown of Open Water Swimming include?

- **A) Three races in Hawaii**

- **B) English Channel, Catalina Channel, Manhattan Island**

- **C) Lake Zurich, Maui Channel, Rottnest Channel**

- **D) Strait of Gibraltar, Alcatraz Swim, English Channel**

Answer: B) English Channel, Catalina Channel, Manhattan Island

3.   What type of swimming is over 10 kilometers in distance?

- A) Sprint swimming

- B) Ice swimming

- C) Marathon swimming

- D) Relay swimming

Answer: C) Marathon swimming

Chapter 18: Fun and Unique Swimming Facts

Fun Facts

1.   Swimming is one of the few sports that works almost every muscle.

2.   The first goggles were made from tortoise shells in Persia.

3.   Swimmers sweat in the pool, even if you can't feel it!

4.   Swimmers burn as many calories as runners, with less impact on joints.

5.   Water can absorb up to 90% of body weight, reducing strain.

6.   The fastest swim stroke is the front crawl, or freestyle.

7.   Swimming was first included in the modern Olympics in 1896.

8.   Dolphins inspired the creation of the butterfly stroke.

9.   Swimmers hold their breath underwater, sometimes up to 30 seconds.

10.   The average Olympic pool holds over 660,000 gallons of water.

11.   Blue-colored pools make it easier to see the black lines.

12.   Flip turns were invented in the 1950s to help swimmers move faster.

13.   Sharks and whales are some of nature's best swimmers.

14.   Swimmers race against the clock, not just each other.

15.   The breaststroke is the slowest competitive stroke.

16.   The "freestyle" allows any stroke, but most use the crawl.

17.   Swimming improves flexibility and strength.

18.   Professional swimmers often eat over 6,000 calories a day.

19.   Swimmers in ancient Greece used olive oil as a protective layer.

20.   The longest underwater swim with a single breath is over 800 feet.

21.   Swimmers practice "sculling" to control hand movements in water.

22.   Swimming is recommended for people of all ages for fitness.

23.   Swimmers can see clearly underwater with goggles.

24.   The Red Sea is known for its warm waters, ideal for swimming.

25.   Swimmers develop special breathing techniques to boost endurance.

End-of-Chapter Quiz

1.   What inspired the creation of the butterfly stroke?

- A) Birds

- B) Fish

- C) Dolphins

- D) Turtles

Answer: C) Dolphins

2.   How many gallons of water does an Olympic pool hold?

- A) 100,000 gallons

- B) 200,000 gallons

- C) 500,000 gallons

- D) 660,000 gallons

Answer: D) 660,000 gallons

3.   What is the fastest competitive stroke?

- A) Breaststroke

- B) Backstroke

- **C) Freestyle**
- **D) Butterfly**

Answer: C) Freestyle

"Is This Book a Real Splash?"

Did this book dive deep into the world of swimming for you, or did it make you float with fun facts? We'd love to hear your thoughts! Whether it broke records or just did a solid lap, your review helps future readers decide if this book deserves a spot on the podium. So, take the plunge and let us know if we made a splash or just a ripple!

Click or scan here

Choose Your Quest: The Dwarven Jester Spy: An Interactive Hilarious High Fantasy Espionage Adventure

Can a jester become a master spy, or will his jokes get him killed?

In this interactive fantasy adventure, YOU take on the role of a quick-witted dwarven jester, secretly hired by the mysterious Group. But what begins as a routine mission quickly spirals into an epic conspiracy that could plunge entire kingdoms into chaos. Armed with nothing but your humor, a few tricks up your sleeve, and a sarcastic talking skull, you must navigate political intrigue, treacherous traps, and ridiculous enemies.

Each decision you make takes you down a unique path. Will you outsmart your foes or get caught in a deadly game of lies? You decide! But be warned, one wrong step and the path of the realm (and your life) could hang in the balance.

What's Inside:

- An Epic High-Fantasy World filled with orcs, elves, and dwarves, where humor is your best weapon.
- Hilarious Characters like the sarcastic talking skull and the eccentric figures you meet along the way.
- Multiple Endings depending on the choices you make, giving the book endless replayability.
- Perfect for Fantasy and Comedy Lovers who enjoy interactive, laugh-out-loud storytelling!

Click or scan here

Continue the Choose Your Quest series here

Download The Galaxy of Comedy Series here. It's like sitcom in space!

Get The Ebook

More from the Author

Discover more exciting adventures and life-enhancing tips at chooseyourquest.net. Dive into a world of interactive fantasy storytelling designed to boost your mental resilience and well-being, **directed to teens & adults**. Explore our collection of books and embark on journeys that entertain, educate, and empower you.

- Choose Your Quest to Mental Resilience
- Choose Your Quest to Survive the Island
- Choose Your Quest to Dream World
- Choose Your Quest to Win the Tournament, Part 1
- Choose Your Quest to Win the Tournament, Part 2

I would greatly appreciate your constructive review on Amazon and Goodreads. Your feedback helps other readers interested in mental health support and adventure discover these books.

Children's Books

Step up to the plate and join the action in The Great Baseball Showdown! This heartwarming story follows a group of diverse boys who come together to form an unlikely baseball team. Led by Omar, and his team.

Good for kids ages 6-8, <u>The Great Baseball Showdown</u> teaches valuable lessons about teamwork, friendship, and determination. With exciting baseball action and relatable characters, this story is a home run for young readers!

Join Max the Bear, Lily the Rabbit, Ollie the Owl, and Ziggy the Squirrel on an exciting journey through the forest! **When these four friends discover a mysterious trail, they set out on an adventure that tests their teamwork, problem-solving skills, and courage**. From crossing rivers and helping lost animals to building a secret treehouse and braving a storm, the Forest Crew learns that true friendship means sticking together and helping others. For ages 5 and above.

Join Amira, Zuri, Sofia, and Mei, four adventurous **8-year-old friends**, as they embark on the adventure of a lifetime! When the four best friends stumble upon a mysterious old map in their treehouse, they find themselves caught in the middle of a thrilling treasure hunt. Together, they must follow a series of clues, explore hidden locations around town, and solve riddles to uncover the true treasure. But it's not just gold they're after—this journey will reveal the forgotten stories and history of their hometown, Maplewood.

The Treehouse Detectives: A Mystery Adventure for Kids Ages 6-8: The Case of the Missing Treasure

<u>Daddy, You're My Hero: A Fun and Heartwarming Story About My Adventures with Dad, Laughter, and Noodles!</u>

Daddy, You're My Hero is a heartwarming and funny story about the special bond between a *little Asian girl and her father.* **Told through the eyes of 8-year-old Mei,** this charming tale follows her adventures with her dad as they navigate life's ups and downs with laughter, love, and noodle soup!

Join Max, Zara, and Leo—the brainy bunch—on an exciting **adventure about science, technology, engineering, and math**. The trio of curious and clever siblings teams up to solve mysteries, build gadgets, and crack codes, all while learning important lessons about teamwork and problem-solving.

Good for kids ages 6-8, this adventure-filled book encourages curiosity, critical thinking, and collaboration.

Giggle Gator is a shy little alligator who just wants to fit in with the other animals in the swamp. But every time he tries to talk to his friends, his shyness gets the best of him! With the help of his loving parents and his quirky animal friends, Giggle discovers that his unique giggle might be the key to making new friends and finding his confidence.

Join Giggle, Chuckle the Cheeky Monkey, Penny the Parrot, Barry the Bear, and Lila the Laughing Hyena on a heartwarming and **funny adventure about self-confidence, family, and the power of laughter.** Full of fun, colorful illustrations and easy-to-read text, this story is perfect for **kids ages 6-8** who are learning to overcome their own fears and embrace what makes them special.

Buy or scan here

Uplifting stories for kids 6-8 yr old, <u>HERE</u>

Download Here

FUN SPORTS FACTS FOR KIDS SERIES

444 + Fun Facts for Sports Kids: **Basketball Edition**: Discover Amazing Skills, Slam Dunk Records, Epic Rivalries & So Much More!

<u>Gift it to your child by clicking here or scanning the QR code</u>

444 + Fun Facts for Sports Kids: Winter Sports Edition**: Discover Cool Facts, Epic Slopes, Thrilling Ice Sports & So Much More! (The Ultimate Gift for Winter Sports Fans & Young Readers)?**

Gift it to your child by clicking here or scanning the QR code

Get The Ebook

444 + Fun Facts for Sports Kids: Track & Field Edition: **Discover Record-Breaking Jumps, Fast Sprints, Legendary Athletes & So Much More**

Gift it to your child by clicking here or scanning the QR code

Continue The Sports Fun Facts Series, here

Fun Facts For Sports Kids (7 book series)
Kindle Edition

Do you know a young sports lover who's always hungry for more knowledge?

Whether they're just starting out, a casual fan, or a die-hard sports fanatic, this book series will satisfy their curiosity with a treasure trove of facts and trivia from the world of sports!

Inside each book of the *Fun Facts for Sports Kids* series, readers will discover:

- Hundreds of mind-blowing, fun, and jaw-dropping sports facts and trivia
- Unbelievable insights, from the science behind each sport to tales of epic comebacks, legendary players, and record-breaking feats

Download Here

Made in United States
Troutdale, OR
12/19/2024

26942161R00070